W9-BED-494

The Truth About PRINCESSES

by Nancy Kelly Allen

illustrated by Youngsun Kim

PICTURE WINDOW BOOKS
a capstone imprint

For Vickie

Thanks to our advisers for their expertise,
research, and advice:

Elizabeth Tucker, Ph.D., Professor of English
Binghamton University, Binghamton, New York

Terry Flaherty, Ph.D., Professor of English
Minnesota State University, Mankato

Editors: Shelly Lyons and Jennifer Besel
Designer: Lori Bye
Art Director: Nathan Gassman
Production Specialist: Jane Klenk
The illustrations in this book were created digitally.

Picture Window Books
151 Good Counsel Drive
P.O. Box 669
Mankato, MN 56002-0669
877-845-8392
www.picturewindowbooks.com

Printed in the United States of America in North Mankato, Minnesota.
092009
005618CGS10

 All books published by Picture Window Books
are manufactured with paper containing at least
10 percent post-consumer waste.

Library of Congress Cataloging-in-Publication Data
Allen, Nancy K.
The truth about princesses / written by Nancy Kelly Allen ;
illustrated by Youngsun Kim.
p. cm. — (Fairy-tale superstars)
Includes index.
ISBN 978-1-4048-5747-6 (library binding)
1. Princesses—Juvenile literature. I. Youngsun, Kim,
ill. II. Title.
GT5350.A44 2010
391'.022—dc22
2009030072

Twinkling Princesses

Hear ye! Hear ye! Calling all princesses! You are invited to the King's Ball at the Royal Castle!

Beautiful princesses in fancy gowns seem to float around in stories. They put on shiny jewelry that makes them twinkle like stars. They live and play all around the world.

3

So are princesses real? Yes, some are real. There are women in different countries of the world who are called princesses. They are members of royal families.

But the princesses in fairy tales are not real. They are make-believe princesses. They live in exciting, magical worlds.

Who is a princess? A princess is the daughter of a king or queen. She could also be the wife of a prince.

Fairy-tale princesses live in times past. Their homes are large castles or big, beautiful buildings. Their kingdoms are in lands far, far away.

What Do Princesses Look Like?

Fairy-tale princesses are almost always beautiful. They have bright eyes and rosy cheeks.

Make-believe princesses love to dress up. They tie ribbons in their hair. They wear jeweled crowns on their heads. Their puffy gowns are made of velvet, silk, lace, and jewels.

In fairy tales, most princesses have long hair. Rapunzel's hair is so long, it reaches down the tall castle tower. Many princesses have hair that looks like gold. Some princesses, such as Snow White, have hair as black as coal.

crown

ribbon

bright eyes

rosy cheeks

jewels

puffy gown

long hair

9

What Do Princesses Do for Fun?

Like many real girls, make-believe princesses enjoy singing and playing with toys. In *The Frog Prince*, the princess loves to play with her golden ball. When she loses the ball, a frog brings it back to her.

Fairy-tale princesses dance the night away at royal balls. In the story *The Twelve Dancing Princesses*, sisters dance so long, they wear holes in their shoes.

Princesses and Problems

The lives of make-believe princesses are filled with more than pretty dresses, playing, and dancing. Princesses face many problems, too.

Sometimes magic gets a princess into trouble. A talking mirror tells an evil queen where Snow White lives.

Other times, magic frees a make-believe princess from trouble. In *The Goose Girl*, a princess is forced to tend to geese. Her talking horse is taken away, but his head is put up on a wall. The horse helps the Goose Girl become a princess once more.

Fairy Magic

Fairy magic can be dangerous. But it can also be helpful. In one story, an angry fairy places a spell on a baby named Sleeping Beauty. The fairy says Sleeping Beauty will die at age 16. But a good fairy quickly changes the spell. Instead of dying, Sleeping Beauty goes into a deep sleep. Later, a kiss from a prince awakens her.

Witches

Witches stir up evil spells for some make-believe princesses. In *The Frog Princess*, a witch turns a girl into a frog. A prince finds the frog, marries her, and helps change her into a princess.

Godmothers and Stepmothers

In the famous story *Cinderella*, a fairy godmother waves her magic wand. Poof! Cinderella's rags change into a beautiful gown. Her dirty shoes become tiny glass slippers.

In some stories, princesses live with mean stepmothers. Some stepmothers make the princesses work from morning until night. Others are worse. They send the princesses into the deep, dark woods to try to keep them from returning home.

Kind Princesses

Fairy-tale princesses are not only beautiful, but they are kind, too. Many treat animals well. One girl kisses a frog before she finds her prince and becomes a princess.

In *Beauty and the Beast*, a girl is nice to a strange beast. She marries the beast. Her kindness breaks the magic spell. Poof! The beast changes into a prince, and the girl becomes a princess.

Smart Princesses

Fairy-tale princesses are smart. They think their way out of trouble. In *Rumplestiltskin*, a princess must guess a man's name or he will steal her child.

Fairy-tale princesses are also brave. In the story *The Dragon Slayer*, a dragon threatens to eat a princess. But the princess never gives up hope.

26

At the beginning of a fairy tale, we see the beauty of the princess. But in the end, we learn her kindness and clever thinking is more important than her beauty. And then the princess finds love and lives happily ever after.

Fun Facts About Princesses

- If you happen to meet a real princess, you should call her "Your Highness."

- Cinderella is one of the oldest fairy-tale princesses. Nearly 2,000 years ago, the ancient Egyptians told a Cinderella story. The Egyptian Cinderella was called Rhodopis.

- Charles Perrault wrote the story *Sleeping Beauty*. The Brothers Grimm later told the same story. Their name for the princess was Briar Rose.

- Each time a fairy tale is told or written, the story changes. In some versions of *The Frog Prince*, the princess does not want to be near the frog. In other versions, the princess kisses the frog. In both versions, the frog becomes a prince.

Glossary

carriage—a fancy buggy pulled by horses

clever—smart

castle—a large house usually made of stone

gown—fancy dress

make-believe—not real

velvet—soft cloth used to make dresses

Index

To Learn More

More Books to Read

Blackaby, Susan. *The Princess and the Pea.* Minneapolis: Picture Window Books, 2004.

Eilenberg, Max. *Cinderella.* Cambridge, Mass.: Candlewick Press, 2008.

McCole, Danielle. *The Classic Treasury of Grimm's Fairy Tales.* Philadelphia: Courage Books, 2001.

Internet Sites

FactHound offers a safe, fun way to find Internet sites related to this book. All of the sites on FactHound have been researched by our staff.

Here's all you do:

Visit *www.facthound.com*

FactHound will fetch the best sites for you!

Look for all of the books in the Fairy-Tale Superstars series:

The Truth About Dragons

The Truth About Fairies

The Truth About Princesses

The Truth About Trolls